Contents

Ready for anything!

Animals are **engineered** by nature to survive in their environments. They have special features that have developed over time. These are called **adaptations**.

DID YOU KNOW?

The fennec fox is the smallest fox in the world, but it has huge ears! Its big ears help it lose body heat. This keeps the fox cool in the hot desert.

Animal Adaptations

Raintree is an imprint of Capstone Global Library Limited, a company incorporated in England and Wales having its registered office at 264 Banbury Road, Oxford, OX2 7DY – Registered company number: 6695582

www.raintree.co.uk
myorders@raintree.co.uk

Originated by Capstone Global Library Ltd
Printed and bound in India

978 1 4747 0047 0 (hardback)
978 1 4747 0057 9 (paperback)

British Library Cataloguing in Publication Data
A full catalogue record for this book is available from the British Library.

Acknowledgements
We would like to thank the following for permission to reproduce photographs: Matt Cornish/ Shutterstock, front cover, pp. 1, 26–27; Hagit Berkovich/ Shutterstock, pp. 4–5; Jez Bennett/ Shutterstock, pp. 6–7; VasylOxi/ Shutterstock, p. 7 (top); Joe McDonald / Steve Bloom Images/ Alamy, pp. 8–9; Stu's Images/ Wikipedia, pp. 10–11; Mady MacDonald/ Shutterstock, p. 13; Joe McDonald/ Shutterstock, pp. 14–15; Gail Johnson/ Shutterstock, p. 15 (middle); James Rosindell/ Wikipedia, pp. 16–17; Sphinx Wang/ Shutterstock, p. 18–19; Amir A/ Shutterstock, p. 20 (bottom); Beth Swanson/ Shutterstock, pp. 20–21; Audrey Snider-Bell/ Shutterstock, pp. 22–23; Phichet Chaiyabin/ Shutterstock, pp. 24–25; Steve Bower/ Shutterstock, pp. 28–29.

A fennec fox's fur keeps it warm during cool nights in the desert.

Some adaptations are shared by many animals. Others are more unusual. Some animals have unique body parts. These help them do amazing things, such as see in the dark. Others have features that make them seem to disappear! Some animals also have surprising ways to avoid predators.

Elephant's trunk

An elephant does not just use its trunk to breathe. It uses this handy body part to find food. When it spots some tasty leaves growing high in a tree, it stretches its long trunk upwards.

There are two pointed tips at the end of its trunk. These work like fingers. The elephant uses these "fingers" to pluck a single leaf from the tree.

Then it curls its flexible trunk and stuffs the food into its mouth!

DID YOU KNOW?

An elephant can use its trunk like a snorkel. It holds the tip above the water. Then it can breathe while it is under water.

Flying squirrel's extra skin

A flying squirrel does not really fly. It **glides**. To get from one tree to another, it climbs high then leaps into the air. It spreads its arms and legs out wide. This makes the loose extra skin between them stretch tight.

The extra skin catches the air. This slows the squirrel's fall. The animal uses its tail as a **rudder** to steer through the air.

Plonk! The squirrel lands safely. Its extra skin loosens, and the squirrel scurries off.

FAST FACT

Gliding between trees helps a flying squirrel avoid predators on the ground.

DID YOU KNOW?

Flying squirrels can glide for 50 metres (165 feet) or more between trees!

extra skin

Engineering in Practice

A flying squirrel's extra skin works like a parachute. Try making your own parachute!

- Cut a large circle out of a paper or plastic bag.
- Punch four holes around the edge of the circle. The holes need to be spaced an equal distance apart.
- Tie string to each hole. Each string should be the same length.
- Tie a toy figure to the ends of the strings under the parachute.
- Test the parachute by dropping it from a high place!

Thorny devil's spines

The thorny devil lives in the hot, dry desert. There, it is hard to find water to drink. But the thorny devil's **spines** help it get the water it needs to survive.

DID YOU KNOW?

The thorny devil's spines are very sharp. They help protect the lizard from predators.

spine

FAST **FACT**

Thorny devils snack on thousands of tiny black ants in a single day.

In the morning, this lizard rubs up against plants. Drops of dew from the plants collect on its spiky back.

These drops run along tiny grooves between the spines. The spines and grooves carry the water straight into the thirsty lizard's mouth!

Tarsier's eyes

High in a tree, a tarsier hunts at night. Its giant, bulging eyes collect what light there is. It can see well even when the moon is behind clouds.

The tarsier watches a cockroach scurrying along a branch. Its round eyes follow the **prey** until it gets close. Then the tarsier leaps forward to grab its snack.

While it eats, the tarsier's big eyes scan the forest. They watch for snakes and other predators.

DID YOU KNOW?

A tarsier has flexible neck bones. They allow it to turn its head 180 degrees in each direction. When sitting in one place, it can spot prey all around!

FAST FACT

Each of a tarsier's eyes is as big and as heavy as its brain!

Walrus's tusks

The cold **Arctic** sea looks flat and calm. Suddenly, a brown head pokes above the water. It is a walrus with huge, white **tusks**!

FAST FACT

A walrus's tusks can grow up to 1 metre (3 feet) long.

The walrus has been feeding in the icy sea. Now it wants to climb onto the ice to soak up the sun.

The walrus lifts its head. It jabs its tusks into the smooth, slippery ice. It then pulls itself up onto the ice. Now it is time for a snooze!

DID YOU KNOW?

The walrus also uses its tusks to drag its body across the ice. It uses them to fight other walruses, too!

Leafy sea dragon's camouflage

In a patch of drifting seaweed, not all is what it seems. One piece of seaweed is actually a leafy sea dragon! This animal gets its name from the leaf-like parts that grow on its body.

The delicate "leaves" look like pieces of wavy seaweed. This camouflage tricks predators! They cannot spot the sea dragon hidden among the seaweed.

The sea dragon swims slowly. This makes it even less likely to catch the eyes of a hungry predator.

ACTIVITY

Engineering in Practice

Animals use colour and shape for camouflage. Try this activity to see how it works.

- Collect about 30 paper clips in different colours.
- Go outside into a grassy area. (Check with an adult first!)
- Spread out the paper clips in the grass. Which colour is easiest to see in the grass? Which is the hardest?

DID YOU KNOW?

Leafy sea dragons' relatives, weedy sea dragons, are red with yellow spots. Weedy sea dragons live among thicker, darker seaweeds.

Flatfish's shape

A flatfish glides along the ocean floor. It stops and buries its flat, thin body in the sand. It uses its fins to throw sand over its body.

The flatfish is covered in brown spots. This colouring helps it to blend in with the sand.

DID YOU KNOW?

Baby flatfish have eyes on each side of their bodies. The eyes shift to one side as they grow.

The flatfish's eyes peek out from its hiding place. They spot a small fish swimming by. The fish does not see the camouflaged flatfish. In a flash, the flatfish lunges, snatching the prey in its mouth!

FAST FACT

Some flatfish can change colour. This also helps them blend in with their surroundings.

Pufferfish's inflation

A pufferfish swims slowly through the water. Suddenly, it sees a large, hungry fish swimming towards it. It cannot get away in time!

The pufferfish quickly sucks in mouthfuls of water. This **inflates** its stretchy stomach. It gets much bigger. The pufferfish is suddenly the shape of a ball!

Pufferfish contain deadly poison. Most predators that eat the fish are killed instantly!

As the pufferfish blows up, flat spikes on its body pop out. The hungry fish is surprised and threatened by this spiky ball. So, it swims away!

DID YOU KNOW?

Pufferfish can grow three times bigger when they are threatened.

Scorpion's tail

spike

A scorpion chases a small lizard. It grabs the lizard in its huge **pincers**, but its prey struggles to escape. The scorpion quickly curls its tail forward and jabs the lizard.

There is a sharp, hollow spike at the end of the scorpion's tail. This spike injects **venom** into the lizard. The powerful venom kills small animals or **paralyses** larger ones.

The venom keeps the lizard from moving. It is time for the scorpion to eat!

DID YOU KNOW?

Even newborn scorpions have venom. They can be just as dangerous as adults!

A scorpion's body is covered in hard plates that protect it from most predators.

pincers

23

Grasshopper's legs

Beetles, birds and mice try to eat grasshoppers. But a grasshopper's extra-long back legs help it escape danger. They work like tiny **catapults**!

FAST FACT

Grasshoppers make sounds by rubbing their back legs against their wings.

The grasshopper uses its leg **muscles** to bend its knees. This tightens parts called cuticles inside the knees. The cuticles squash like **springs**. They store up energy.

When it wants to jump, the grasshopper relaxes its muscles. The cuticles spring open, and the grasshopper launches into the air!

DID YOU KNOW?

A grasshopper can jump 20 times the length of its body!

Frilled lizard's frill

A frilled lizard walks along the ground. Suddenly, it spots a predator!

The lizard stands tall on its back legs. It opens its mouth wide and hisses loudly. Then, whoosh! It opens and raises its huge frill. This large piece of loose skin usually hangs over its shoulders like a cape.

The **ribbed** frill makes the lizard look much bigger. It scares most enemies away!

FAST FACT

The frilled lizard's frill is 30 centimetres (12 inches) across.

frill

DID YOU KNOW?

Frilled lizards spend most of their time in trees. They scan the ground for insects and other small animals to eat. Then they run after prey on their two back legs.

ACTIVITY

Engineering in Practice

Take a close look at an umbrella to see how the frilled lizard opens its frill!

- When the umbrella is closed, the folds of fabric lie flat.
- When you open the umbrella, the ribs in the umbrella open out.
- This unfolds the fabric and stretches it tight. This makes the umbrella much bigger.
- This is how the frilled lizard's frill works, too!

27

Engineered to survive

Why do animals have these amazing adaptations? Unique body parts such as the flying squirrel's extra skin help it to glide from tree to tree. The walrus's huge tusks help it to grip slippery ice.

DID YOU KNOW?

An armadillo has bony plates covering its back, head, legs and tail. It looks like a suit of armour! The plates protect it from bears, foxes and other predators.

To defend itself, an armadillo tucks its head and tail in, then rolls into a ball!

Camouflage helps the leafy sea dragon hide from predators. It helps the flatfish catch prey. The pufferfish's ability to blow itself up into a spiky ball scares off enemies. Without these amazing adaptations, these animals would not be able to survive.

Glossary

adaptations features or characteristics that an organism has that help it to survive

Arctic region around the North Pole

camouflage colours or patterns that help an animal to blend in with its surroundings

catapults machines that use tension to launch objects

dew tiny drops of water that form on cool surfaces at night

engineered designed and built

glide carried by the wind

grooves deep, narrow spaces

inflate blows up with air or water

muscles body parts that make animals move, for example, by pulling on animal bones

paralyse stop an animal from moving

pincers special claws

predators animals that catch and eat other animals

prey animals eaten by other animals

ribbed having longer structures that support something

rudder flat piece of wood or metal on a boat or plane that is moved to steer the vehicle

spines sharp body parts that stick out

springs coils of metal that bounce back after you squash them down and let them go

tusks special, long pointed teeth

venom poison produced by some animals

Find out more

BOOKS

Amazing Animal Shape-Shifters (Animal Scientists), Leon Gray
(Raintree, 2016)

Animal! The Animal Kingdom as You've Never Seen it Before
(Knowledge Encyclopedia), DK (DK Children, 2016)

Animals That Dig (Adapted to Survive), Angela Royston (Raintree, 2014)

WEBSITES

www.bbc.co.uk/bitesize/topics/zvhhvcw/articles/zxg7y4j
Learn more about adaptation.

www.dkfindout.com/uk/animals-and-nature
Find out more about animals and nature.

Index